MOURNING INTO DANCING

MY JOURNEY THROUGH SEPARATION AND DIVORCE

WANDA ROBINSON

3rd Edition

ISBN: 9798511600253

Imprint: Independently published

Illustrated by: WANDA K ROBINSON

Contents

Dear Friend,

There is a season for everything. In this book, I want to share some nuggets of wisdom that God has given to me on my journey through separation and divorce. Many people have come to me on this path. Each one brought a different nugget at a specific time when I needed it. Father God knows when I need a song, a shoulder to cry or lean on, a listening ear, or a message that is shared with me.

The purpose of writing *Mourning into Dancing* is to encourage and touch others with hope. If you are on a journey or in a season, keep your heart open to the people that God brings your way. They may have a nugget to share.

I want you to know that you are never alone in your darkness or despair. No matter how overwhelmed or helpless you may be, God is walking with you. Do not push away God, or the people He brings, by thinking you can handle your situation on your own. Embrace the truths they bring. They have been specifically and strategically sent to you. You do not have to stay in your mourning season. You can move on and dance. You will laugh again.

So, grab your coffee, settle into a chair in the sunshine, and begin reading. Wanda Robinson

I REFUSE TO BE SILENT

I **REFUSE TO BE SILENT** about the happenings in my life, whether they are good or bad!

I WILL NOT BE Silent

THE ENEMY STOLE my husband and children from me, through the dissolution of my marriage, and thinks that he has won.

NO, IT IS A LIE!

My God is *greater* and more *powerful* than any mere attack or attempt of the enemy!

My Father God holds me in the palm of His hand.

> Isaiah 49:15,16
>
> :15 Can a woman forget her nursing child, and not have compassion on the son of her womb? Surely, they may forget, yet I will not forget you.
>
> :16 See, I have inscribed you on the palms of My hands; your walls are continually before Me.

> Isaiah 50:4-10
>
> :4 The LORD God has given Me the tongue of the learned, that I should know how to speak a word in season to him who is weary. He awakens Me morning by morning; He awakens My ear to hear as the learned.
>
> :5 The LORD God has opened My ear; and I was not rebellious, nor did I turn away.
>
> :6 I gave My back to those who struck Me, and My cheeks to those who plucked out the beard; I did not hide My face from shame and spitting.
>
> :7 For the LORD God will help Me; therefore I will not be disgraced; therefore I have set My face like a flint, and I know that I will not be ashamed.
>
> :8 He is near who justifies Me; who will contend with Me? Let us stand together. Who is my adversary? Let him come near Me.

*:9a Surely, the LORD God will help Me; Who is he who will
condemn Me?*

*:10 Who among you fears the Lord? Who obeys the voice of
His Servant? Who walks in darkness and has no light? Let
him trust in the name of the LORD and rely upon his God.*

Isaiah 43:19
*Behold I will do a new thing, now it shall spring forth; shall you
not know it?*

I THANK the Lord for this passage of scripture. It shows me how God is so great
and powerful, yet so loving.

I draw from His *truths,* which are promises of hope, peace, encouragement,
stability, strength, blessings, a future, freedom, wholeness...and I could go on
for a while. I am sure I would be quite lost without His Word!

PSALMS 30:11-12

You have turned for me my mourning into dancing; You have put off my
sackcloth and clothed me with gladness, to the end that my glory may sing
praise to You and not be silent.

Mourning: crying, weeping, sorrow, hurt, and pain.

Dancing: happy, joyful, excitement.

Sackcloth: observed when a person wears mourning clothes.
(Usually black colored clothing).

Gladness: joy, exhilaration, and or cheerfulness.

Glory: understood as--my tongue and or my soul may sing praise to God.

3

NOTES   Ideas   THOUGHTS

THE

LORD GOD

WILL

HELP

ME AND YOU!

TO EVERYTHING THERE IS A SEASON

To Everything There Is a Season,

> *A time for every purpose under heaven:*
> *A time to be born, and a time to die; a time to plant, and a time*
> *to pluck what is planted; a time to kill, and a time to heal; a*
> *time to break down, and a time to build up;*
> *A time to weep, and a time to laugh; A time to mourn, and a*
> *time to dance. Ecclesiastes 3:1- 4*

MOURNING

> *Isaiah 61:3*
> *To console those who mourn in Zion, to give them beauty for*
> *ashes, the oil of joy for mourning, the garment of praise for*
> *the spirit of heaviness; that they may be called trees of*
> *righteousness, the planting of the LORD, that He may be*
> *glorified.*

OFTEN, this word is associated with a loved one passing away—death —a funeral.

At a funeral, the immediate family is involved with all the aspects involving the funeral: arrangements, the memorial service, flowers, luncheon, and the list goes on. They also need to find the grace to be able to hold themselves together to converse with the guests who have come to pay their last respects. If you have had someone pass on, then you understand the burden that the immediate family must carry.

A separation or divorce is a *breakdown* within the marriage between the husband and wife. There is mourning, whether the marriage has lasted two or twenty years.

Do not deny yourself time to mourn. The only way to heal is to mourn. There is no possible way to jump from stage one to stage four of the grieving process. Every stage must be gone through to properly heal!

After all, if a person had surgery following a heart attack and had a pacemaker put in, we would not be seeing him or her jumping up the next day and attempting to go for a jog.

HEALING MUST TAKE PLACE

At the beginning of my journey, I mourned, grieved, cried, lay in ashes (despair), and asked God *"why?"* over and over. There was a season—a time for that.

I kept pushing forward. It was the only way I could keep my head above water while attempting to swim with absolutely no energy. I had to survive, even if I had no idea how to. There were so many things that needed my immediate attention, and there were so many arrows pointing all sorts of directions. Finding the right arrow was a challenge. One part of me wanted to crawl under the blankets and stay there until things changed, but there was a small part that had to keep moving, breathing, and finding solutions to the hundreds of questions that needed answers.

So many challenges! After I would tackle one situation and achieve success, the next situations were not as daunting. In the middle of mourning, I was learning and becoming stronger. It still was a hard journey, and many times I wanted to jump off the boat and give up, but I resisted.

The enemy would come with lies or would try to put fear in me. Sometimes he would come with thoughts of suicide, and depression would settle on me. The best solution I found for this was going for a walk outside, in the bitter cold if I had to. The fresh air was good and refreshing, and while out I could see clearly what the enemy was trying to put in my head. On my return to the warmth of my place, I would reach for my Bible to fill my soul with His Truths and listen to anointed praise and worship.

One very important area that I want to emphasize is that you must surround yourself with people who love you for who you are (no matter what others might say about you), believe in you, and support you.

Be careful and wise in choosing who you want to confide in. I had many people who said they wanted to help me. Often, there were those who were still dealing with hurt, anger, and bitterness from their own situations and experiences. That was too much for me. I had to let those people go. I did not have the energy to listen to their stories. I found that it drained me, and I needed to conserve all my effort for my own self, at that part of my journey.

Others had so many questions that it seemed I was repeating my story over and over. The more I told my story, the angrier and more frustrated I became, because I was rehashing it repeatedly. Not everyone needs to know every detail of your pain or situation. Pray and ask God to show you who to choose to talk to. Some people will be offended because you do not pick them. Do not worry about those ones!

NOTES   Ideas   THOUGHTS

BEAUTY

for ashes

The OIL OF JOY

for mourning

The GARMENT OF PRAISE

for the spirit of heaviness...

SUPPORT SYSTEM

Early in my journey of separation, I went to see a counsellor for help. She assisted me in showing me how to select people to help. It is very important to be selective. Often when we are hurting, a tendency is to grab anyone that will listen.

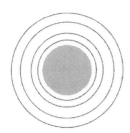 THIS DIAGRAM DEMONSTRATES how to choose and place people for the various stages that we go through during a crisis or just in general. It is beneficial to have this operational all through life.

Center dot: 1–2 very close people to confide in.

First circle: 2–4 people you can trust and lean on, who are not affected by your separation/divorce.

Second circle: 5–10 people—a support group—to share with, unload on, cry, and laugh with.

Third circle: 11–15 friends and acquaintances that you can let your hair down with.

Fourth circle: 20–25 people you interact with casually who may or may not be aware of your situation: church members, doctor, mechanic, co-workers.

Get involved in a support group. I highly recommend DivorceCare (www.divorcecare.org). This is a thirteen-week program with a faith-based support group, held in a church.

I am so grateful for this support group. It included a video presentation and then discussion time. Hearing others confide about their problems helped me unload and be able to trust again. This group allowed us to cry, which enabled us to heal. I gained precious friends through this support group.

DivorceCare has "One Day at a Time," daily e-mails. These e-mails are an excellent source of encouragement. They helped me so much during the first two years of my separation. I can recall many times when I was going through something and I clicked on the e-mail, and it was exactly what I needed to read.

A support group is so beneficial to have as you progress down the path of your journey. The more you hold your hurts and issues in, the more they build, and they may eventually erupt like a volcano. Holding things in also leads you to stay in the mourning season longer than you should.

Believe

and

Hope

NOTES Ideas THOUGHTS

FEEL LIKE A VICTIM

Often, people try to "fix" you or "advise" you in your situation.

A FEW PEOPLE tried that with me. Oh, probably in their heart they meant well, but it really bothered me and made me feel lower than them. It was like they thought they would get brownie points for their offer of help. I do not want to sound sarcastic, but this is reality. When someone dies or divorces, we do not know what the pat answer is, so we mumble something. It really is how life is. (Some people do have appropriate answers or solutions).

THERE IS no manual for separation and divorce.

Do not be pressured by anyone to do something. Make sure it is God telling you to do things; otherwise, you may find yourself frustrated.

During the first year of my separation my inner self was very weak and vulnerable, and I had trust issues. A couple of people tried to help me, but I found myself frustrated each time after being with them. I encourage you to find people who flow by the Spirit of the Lord, and confide in and unload on them—even if it takes five hours.

IT IS VERY important to find a prayer pal/partner.

Not only do you need to share with someone, but prayer is key. Knowing that a person is praying for you is the number one booster! At times, especially at night when I was all alone, I would ask God to put me on someone's heart to pray. I have told people who are going through these experiences to simply text me, *"pray,"* and I will. I do not need to know the situation or reason. God knows. I will do my part by praying.

I also discovered a form of therapy for myself: I walked a lot my first year. I would push myself to walk farther and find new places. I would not take my vehicle and would walk, even in bitterly cold weather.

Other therapy that helped included holding a baby, petting a cat or dog, digging in the dirt, doing a new activity I had often wanted to tackle, taking an evening class, or volunteering in a senior's home

Have you found a "therapy" or something that helps you get through?

Do you like the "challenge" of doing something new to you?

Often a new challenge helps our minds to focus on a different aspect than on our current situation.

NOTES Ideas THOUGHTS

PSALMS 23

The LORD is my shepherd; I shall not want.

> *:2 He makes me to lie down in green pastures; He leads me*
> *beside the still waters.*
> *:3 He restores my soul; He leads me in paths of righteousness*
> *for His name's sake.*
> *:4 Yea, though I walk through the valley of the shadow of*
> *death, I will fear no evil; For you are with me; Your rod and*
> *Your staff, they comfort me.*
> *:5 You prepare a table before me in the presence of my*
> *enemies; You anoint my head with oil; my cup runs over.*
> *:6 Surely goodness and mercy will follow me all the days of my life;*
> *and I will dwell in the house of the LORD. Forever.*

THE SHEPHERD

Mourning into Dancing

It seems the days that are very hard are when I reach out to God more.

God as a Shepherd—I hold onto His hand, knowing He will lead and guide me.

God as a Father—I allow Him to make the decisions, knowing that He knows best, and I can completely trust Him.

God as a Husband—He loves me and cherishes me, and I know He will love me even when I make mistakes.

My hardest and lowest moments of despair and anguish came when my husband first told me to leave. I was literally numb. Previously, the road signs had shown that something was going to happen. What I mean by that is that we would pass each other in the hallway as strangers, he slept in the living room, there was increased tension, he ate out more with the guys and did not eat many meals that I cooked.

In no way do I want to make my spouse look like the bad guy. I simply want to tell my side of my story so that Father God can touch, heal, and restore you.

I was not prepared for the blow when it happened. Maybe it was normal to think our difficulties would pass. We had been struggling in our marriage for awhile, but the last year and a half was more intense. We disagreed on various things, mostly pertaining to our preteens and teenagers and choices they wanted to make. We barely communicated or went out as a couple. Is anyone ever prepared for or ready for disaster, death, or the breakdown of a marriage?

Mourning into Dancing

I cried and screamed. I also got in touch with people—family and friends—and asked them to pray for me. I was terrified, scared, and desperately hurting. My spouse's rejection devastated me. The marriage vow kept ringing in my ears. This cannot be happening! This happens to other people, not me! Not us!

Through this very hurtful and awful time, the Shepherd held me close to His heart. He held me and held me. His love overflowed onto me. He saw my tears. One way that the Shepherd showed His closeness to me was by bringing a worship song to me; for instance, I would hear a song on the Christian radio station, and it would minister to me all day. Sometimes He would lead me to a verse in the Bible that would encourage me. I felt the presence of the Lord so strongly, and I knew I was not alone.

My family was gone. My children were not there and did not want to be with me. I had anger issues for many years, and my children were affected by the anger and by the gossip flying around. I felt that they had unforgiveness and bitterness toward me. It all happened too fast, this separation. I was in a whirlwind of despair and could hardly breathe. I blamed myself and the anger I had, for the breakdown of our marriage. I was drowning! How could I forgive myself for the years of anger? How could I undo the damage that had been done?

I had to take steps to forgive myself. It was a process that did not happen overnight. I had to go deep within myself. Once I took those steps of forgiveness, I could move on past the anguish. Yes, I had hurt my husband and family. I could not go back and fix the past, but I could move forward and make changes.

I went to a Christian psychologist who helped me understand why I reacted in certain ways. I discovered what the trigger points were and made changes here and there. One thing that triggered the anger was stress. I must have thought I was Wonder Woman, because each day my task list was very long, and I did not give myself enough time to accomplish things. This then led to frustration and anger.

Also, because there was so much to do within the house, I often would not do anything. I felt overwhelmed by stress and life happenings. Once I allowed myself time to complete a task, the anger died down.

Also, my thinking about what I assumed others expected of me (when perhaps they did not) was a trigger point. For instance, if people were coming to visit, I thought they expected a perfectly clean house, and I usually got a migraine during such stressful times.

I speak of this anger to you in case you or others you know suffer and struggle with anger. I may now understand why my husband drew away from me and was never around. My children stopped having friends over and socialized outside our home. I loved my family very much, but they did not feel loved by me, because of the anger.

Coming to this realization has hurt me tremendously! The Shepherd has come and ministered His peace, presence, joy, forgiveness, and healing to me. I know that I am free from the anguish of what I had been and am free from the dark clutches of despair.

I also know that my anger was visible, yet there were also underlying issues within the marriage. I was not the only one to blame for the breakdown of our marriage.

As days and months passed during that first year of separation, I came to the realization that "it takes two to tango," as the saying goes.

Now I realize that I probably jumped too quickly when my husband said the words "Just leave." I should have waited and mulled things over. But I did not. I began to get things from the house. It felt like a dream, and I was going to wake up—but no, it was not a dream. What does one take from the family home? A friend had suggested that I write down everything I wanted, because with the turmoil, I might forget. The Shepherd was there, holding my hand, leading, guiding, loving, directing, and speaking to me.

When I look back on those first days and months, they feel like a tornado. My husband and family kept functioning as if nothing had happened, yet I knew that all our lives had changed.

THE SHEPHERD NEVER LEFT ME.

See yourself as God Sees You.

I see myself as a stubborn sheep that persisted in going into the rosebush with its pretty-smelling flowers and thorns. My loving Heavenly Father, the Shepherd, would come and pick me up out of the thorns that got stuck in my wool. He would hold me close in His arms and gently pick out all the thorns, and then He would soothe the wounds with His ointment. He would love and not scold me as He restored me back to health. He would take me beside the cool water and the green grass, telling me to rest—to rest my weary soul, mind, and body from the turbulent storm that I had been put into, to rest from the hurts, pain, words, lies, doubts, and darkness.

A SHEPHERD AND HIS SHEEP.

What do a shepherd and sheep do? Sometimes a sheep keeps wandering away into a thicket, or into a thorny bush, or into a dangerous place, and the shepherd tries to correct the sheep by directing it back to the fold.

Possibly this sheep is stubborn and determined to do its own thing, so the shepherd breaks one of its legs and carries the sheep. It gets to know the shepherd's heartbeat and becomes very familiar with his voice and mannerisms.

When the leg has healed, the shepherd puts the sheep down, so it can join the other sheep.

Now the sheep desires to stay close to the shepherd, and any temptation to go elsewhere is gone. It wants to stay close to the shepherd, where it is cared for and loved.

How is your relationship with The Shepherd?

25

Isaiah 53:6

*All we like sheep have gone astray; we have turned everyone,
to his own way; and the LORD has laid on Him the iniquity
of us all.*

1 Peter 2:25

*For you were like sheep going astray, but have now returned
to the Shepherd and Overseer of your souls.*

JESUS IS THE LIGHT IN THE DARKNESS

You have heard the expression "light at the end of the tunnel."

Jesus is the light in the darkness

God showed me that He is with me in the tunnel. This encouraged me so much at the beginning of my journey.

A tunnel can be very long, with twists and turns, and it is dark. As I journey down the long, dark tunnel of life, many issues and situations need my attention, my money, my signature, and my input. It seems like a dark tunnel, and I am exhausted and so ready to be done. But there is a light—Jesus—who walks with me. Together we walk. The way is clearer, and His light is bright.

26

As the song says, "And He walks with me, and He talks with me." I am not alone on this journey.

> *Matthew 6:33*
> *But seek first the kingdom of God and His righteousness, and*
> *all these things shall be added to you.*

> *Philippians 4:13*
> *I can do all things through Christ who strengthens me.*

Seek God first, during turmoil, confusion, stress, darkness, misery, and pain. You can do this! You will get through this! Do not despair! Do not give up!

THE VALLEY OF THE SHADOW OF DEATH

Yea, though I walk through the valley of the shadow of death, I will fear no evil; For you are with me; Your rod and Your staff, they comfort me.
Psalm 23:4

Mourning into Dancing

> A valley: symbolises low moments in our lives, vulnerable moments
>
> - shadow of death—shadows are images of the real thing
> - death lurks in the area and is casting shadows-shadows also depict fearful things.
>
> When we are afraid in dark places, we can start to see shadows.
>
> In a low moment in our life we feel threatened (whether it is our marriage, job, life).
>
> We all pass through low moments in our life, where we see shadows and have a fear of tomorrow.
>
> "I will fear no evil, for You are with me..." An awareness of the presence of God is paramount.
>
> Know, that despite the fear, the shadows, or how we may feel at those moments, that He is still with us."
>
> — PREACHER ROD NGWENYA

SOME DAYS it was so dark, and I could not see my way. I could barely breathe, and the darkness was thick and oppressive. It was very real, and I wanted to get away from the darkness. I wanted to run, but I could not. There was no escape. It was dirty and muddy. My feet were stuck in the mud and mire...no escape...no way out...despair! Lies and evil lurked around every corner.

But I knew in that darkness that I was not alone! The Shepherd was there. I get teary-eyed now, thinking back to that first year. My husband had rejected me. We were supposed to be together...growing old together, watching our children grow up and then enjoying the grandchildren together. But that possibility was gone; dreams were blown apart by the bomb of separation.

Things needed my attention. I needed to see a counsellor, get legal aid, and make some decisions. I needed a place to stay. Things were pressing on me: decisions, thoughts, feelings, accusations, and despair.

I did not choose this separation and divorce. It was chosen for me.

By God's strength **I will** endure. **I will** overcome every obstacle, decision, hurt, and pain, and **I will** have the strength to deal with the legal issues.

NOTES *Ideas* THOUGHTS

GOD AND ME ON A PARK BENCH

One day I was feeling lonely—lonely for my husband, for a companionship that we hardly had in our marriage. I said this to God. Instantly, I felt my head on His shoulder.

THEN GOD GAVE me this picture to recreate. The experience was amazing to me. I was chatting with a sister in the Lord and told her about this. At that time, she had been away from her husband; God had them serving and working in different countries. I sent the picture to her.

Mourning into Dancing

God has shown me repeatedly that, so many people are experiencing or have experienced the same things I have gone through. He wants to use these trying times or uncomfortable situations to help others.

My friend, if you have gone through something, there is a great probability that God will use you to touch or help someone else.

Keep your heart open to the Holy Spirit. Be available, and allow the Holy Spirit to use you.

1 Peter 5:8–10
:8 Be sober, be vigilant; because your adversary the devil walks about like a roaring lion, seeking whom he may devour.
:9 Resist him, steadfast in the faith, knowing that the same sufferings are experienced by your brotherhood in the world.
:10 But may the God of all grace, who called us to His eternal glory by Christ Jesus, after you have suffered a while, perfect, establish, strengthen, and settle you.

Comfort in Suffering

2 Corinthians 1:3-7
:3 Blessed be the God and Father of our Lord Jesus Christ, the Father of mercies and God of all comfort,
:4 who comforts us in all our tribulation, that we may be able to comfort those who are in any trouble, with the comfort with which we ourselves are comforted by God.
:5 For as the sufferings of Christ abound in us, so our consolation also abounds through Christ.
:6 Now if we are afflicted, it is for your consolation and salvation, which is effective for enduring the same sufferings which we also suffer.
:7 And our hope for you is steadfast, because we know that as you are partakers of the sufferings, so also you will partake of the consolation

Perfect   Establish   Strengthen

NOTES   Ideas   THOUGHTS

Mourning into Dancing

WALK WITH ME MY CHILD

When the way gets rough, I will carry you. Trust Me!

WHEN I SAW THIS VISION, I could hear God laughing. It was a low, rumbling laugh. It was wonderful! I was laughing like a little child. We were so content and enjoying our time together at the beach. I was running around, looking at seashells all over the beach, enjoying myself! My bare toes squished in the sand, leaving prints behind. I could sense the sand, the ocean water moving, and the smells of being at the beach—sand, water, and air. It was so exhilarating!

I did not feel God holding my hand, I just knew that He was. And then I felt myself being carried over the rocks. I had assumed that the figure in my vision was God. When I used my pastels to do the picture, I was amazed to see that it was an angel.

I remember asking God, "Can't we stay here?" Later, when I looked at the time, I was totally amazed. God and I had been at the beach for a very long time!

This picture and my description do not even come close to capturing what I experienced. I just love how God loves on me. He knows how much I love being at the ocean. I felt so free and content, just God and me.

I would like to share something that God told me close to the time of the vision at the beach.

THIS IS how God talks to me:

"Watch Me, Wanda; watch Me do it. It is not of your own understanding. I am doing it. Be still. Be patient. Draw close to Me. I am holding you. I see your heart's desire. You have been faithful in the little! Soon you will have much. I am with you.

Never lose sight of Me. I am number one. You have proven to Me that I am number one in your life.

Keep on. Do not struggle with the new things and levels. I will lead and guide you, as I have all these years.

Keep on persevering. You are strong and able and smart. Do not limit yourself. I am your pilot, and you are the co- pilot. I give the directions, and you follow.

My daughter, I love you. Precious daughter.

Let it all go, and run with me. Laugh with me. I have said that you are free and whole. You are! Walk in it! Walk free! You are not shackled or bound anymore. I have set you free; don't question or wonder, just run with Me into the next level, and the next, and the next."

WALKING WITH GOD

NOTES Ideas THOUGHTS

Mourning into Dancing

BE STILL

God has spoken this to me continuously in the more than three years since my separation.

I UNDERSTAND this as God telling me to be quiet, to still my mind, to be at rest.

The best way for me to do this is to go for a nature walk. If that is not possible, then I play worship music.

What does it mean to be still? To be quiet. To calm my mind and thoughts and sit still. To be at peace. To linger in His presence by reading the Bible and worshipping God.

When I am *still*, I can catch my breath; I can stop all the confusion; I can think clearly; I can allow God to show me His will.

Isaiah 26:3
You will keep him in perfect peace, whose mind is stayed on
*   You, because he trusts in You.*

 *BE STILL AND KNOW THAT I AM GOD!*
*   Psalm 46:10 (KJV)*

- *if you are in a pit*
- *have no family*
- *in all circumstances*
- *even though I walk through the valley of the shadow of death*
- *in the midst of the storm*

THEN GOD WILL FULFILL EVERY WORD.
*   The disciples were professional fishermen. There was water and weather; you can tell a good fisherman when he can predict the weather. Yet this was a new storm that rose up.*
*   When life gets you at a sudden moment, BE STILL AND KNOW THAT I AM GOD.*

BE STILL in His presence.
*   That's where I belong. Fear not! Don't be afraid!*
*   The battle is the Lord's.*
*   When you are facing the Red Sea.*
*   BE STILL and know.*
*   Whatsoever—don't lose God—hang on!*
*   Storms and Seasons.*
*   BE STILL and know.*

When the world thinks you would panic or throw things around, and you didn't.

BE STILL! In the midst of trial, fire, and temptation.

BE STILL AND KNOW THAT I AM GOD! STAND STILL AND SEE THE DELIVERANCE OF GOD!" PREACHER ROD NGWENYA

THE LIGHTHOUSE

Some days it feels as if the waves, rain, hail, and lightning are constantly hitting me.

THIS IS LIFE—MAYBE more so when one is going through a major life trauma (death, separation and/or divorce).

The image of the *lighthouse* is soothing. I know that life will hit me with all it can, and I am safe and secure within the *lighthouse*.

God my Father, my Maker...
Jesus Christ, my Lighthouse...
Holy Spirit, my Comforter...

Darts, arrows, lies, accusations, judgment, and whatever is thrown at me, by people (friends, workmates, relatives).

I am safe from their dirty looks, unanswered e-mails, and phone calls.

Psalm 18:1-3
I will love You, O LORD, my strength.
:2 The LORD is my rock and my fortress and my deliverer; my God, my strength, in whom I will trust; my shield and the horn of my salvation, my stronghold.

:3 I will call upon the LORD, who is worthy to be praised; so shall I be saved from my enemies.

Proverbs 18:10 The name of the LORD is a strong tower; the righteous run to it and are safe.

BE STILL

AND KNOW THAT

HE IS GOD!!

What do you do to be still?
What helps to quiet your mind from all that is going on?
Do you have a place that you like to go to be still?
Have you found God to be a rock and fortress?

NOTES **Ideas** **THOUGHTS**

Mourning into Dancing

PRAYER IS THE KEY

Prayer is the key... keep seeking God.

WE HAVE GROWN up in a society that has disillusioned us.

We were informed, mostly by the media, that we would meet and marry Mr. Right, who would be tall, dark, and handsome. Our home would be surrounded by a white picket fence, and everything would be cozy and rosy. It truly is a fairy tale!

45

We are not perfect, so how can our mate be perfect? We do not have all the answers, so how can our mate answer all our questions?

People place high demands and expectations on a marriage. Oh, why is our every whim and desire not being met? What happened to the dating days and honeymoon bliss?

Where have we put God?

MAN   WOMAN

It is very important to have a relationship with our heavenly Father as a single individual. When we allow this to blossom, grow, and mature, we benefit. Once this relationship with our Heavenly Father is established, then we may pursue a mate.

As we come together as a husband and wife, our priorities are in place, and we will continue walking hand in hand with Jesus. He is Lord and should be Lord of every area of our life.

ROOTED IN HIM

BUILT UP IN HIM

STABLISHED IN THE FAITH

ABOUNDING WITH THANKSGIVING

Colossians 2:6,7
As you therefore have received Christ Jesus
the Lord, so walk in Him,
rooted and built up in Him and established in
the faith, as you have been taught,
abounding in it with thanksgiving.

OUR ROOTS ARE FOUNDED in Him. He is the way. We are walking in His truth!

**I am an empty vessel
to be filled by
only You.**

**FILL
me
LORD!**

ONLY FATHER GOD can completely fill this empty spot.

Husband, children, or family cannot even attempt to fill this. Now that I am on this side of my separation and no longer a part of my family, I realize more now that having a husband and family is very important.

But I want to make a point here: only Father God can fill you up. He can fill every ache and hole left from a separation or divorce. People were not created to do this. They are incapable of doing this *completely*, and that is because only God can. Only Father God can see the hole inside you. Only He can see and understand the emotions you are going through.

Only God can.

Father God never moves away from us or leaves us or forsakes us. *We* move away from Him. I cannot do anything on my own; I need Him to empower me. I am nothing in my own strength.

Philippians 4:13

48

Mourning into Dancing

I can do all things through Christ who strengthens me.

I have been going to church since before I was born, and one thing I still cherish are the old hymns we sang. They are still a joy to listen to and sing along with. "I Surrender All" is one hymn that comes to me often. Many years ago, in Bible college, our choir sang this song.
We practiced so often that we heard the words in our dreams.

I SURRENDER

Reality check: surrendering oneself is not achieved through words alone. There is action that must take place. As I *let go and let God,* I have had to *surrender all* to Father God. Some days I longed to be able to just voice the words or sing them and not have to put action to my words.

When I say, "I surrender, Lord," I am allowing God to do what He wants. I let go. I realize that I am empty. I surrender my desire to be reunited with my husband and family.

I surrender the dream of having a house out in the country and all my grandchildren coming to play. I surrender my dreams. I have areas of my life that are not pleasing to God. I may not be sinning outright (like robbing a bank or lying), but there are things that God wants me to surrender. The main reason He wants that is, so I will become more like Him. He is my Father, and He wants me, His daughter, to reflect Him in everything I am and everything I do. He has a plan and purpose for my life, and Father God knows how I need Him in every area

OUR HEAVENLY FATHER IS A JEALOUS GOD.

He wants *all* of us. We need to *surrender all*.

God does not want to share us, especially with anger, hatred, bitterness, envy, and unforgiveness.

We are like a child carrying a bundle that is too heavy. It is full of *"baggage"* that is unnecessary, unimportant, heavy, and burdening.

Solution: we should lay all that down at the cross, and leave it there!

As we place the bundle at Jesus's feet at the cross, we become *free*!

Exodus 20:1-6

And God spoke all these words, saying:

:2 "I am the Lord your God, who brought you out of the land of Egypt, out of the house of bondage.

:3 "You shall have no other gods before Me.

:4 "You shall not make for yourself a carved image—any likeness of anything that is in heaven above, or that is in the earth beneath, or that is in the water under the earth;

:5 you shall not bow down to them nor serve them. For I, the Lord your God, am a jealous God, visiting the iniquity of the fathers upon the children to the third and fourth generations of those who hate Me,

:6 but showing mercy to thousands, to those who love Me and keep My commandments.

NOW, WE ARE LIBERATED AND ABLE TO DANCE!

NOTES Ideas THOUGHTS

EVENING AT THE LAKE

One day I had been praising and worshipping God and then felt the urge to be quiet.

GOD THEN TOOK me to this scene. In a vision. I was at a lake. It was evening, and the moonlight lit up the beach area where I was walking. I could feel my feet in the sand and feel the cool breeze. I smelled different scents, heard the night sounds of frogs and birds and the water gently moving.

It was so beautiful. I know my picture does not do it justice, because I am not sure I could capture what I felt and sensed.

It was just God and me at the lake, and I felt completeness, wholeness, and security.

It was nighttime, with no one else there...just me and Father God.

⌒

Just Be You!

We are not *being* who we really are!
Leave the reasoning and figuring out behind.
God established you to shine for His Glory!
Just Be...
not **what** everyone else wants you to be; —Be
who God wants you to be.
—Be **where** God wants you to be.
—Leave all the questions of **why** to God.
As a child runs to Daddy for reassurance and love, let us
eagerly run into Father God's arms.
He is waiting for us.
We are cherished and loved **Unconditionally!**

NOTES Ideas THOUGHTS

Mourning into Dancing

GOD'S POCKET

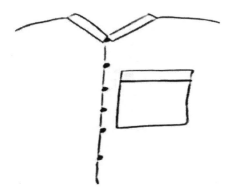

So, it is You and me, eh, Papa God.

God and I are on a team together. I will put my husband in God's pocket for God to take care of and deal with. Then, I will work on me. This journey is daunting and there are so many struggles. The pain of separation and rejection is overwhelming and there are new territories to tackle.

Oh Lord help me... I hurt so much...it is so unbearable.

But you are *always* with me.

1 Peter 5:6,7

:6 Therefore humble yourselves under the mighty hand of
God, that He may exalt you in due time,
:7 casting all your care upon Him, for He cares for you.

Only God has access to His own pocket. It is best I leave my husband there; then I will stop strangling him. He is not mine to dictate or control...that's God's job.

The idea behind this picture of God's Pocket came from my aunt during my first year of separation from my husband, marriage, and family.

That first year, I experienced a lot of hurt, anger, disappointment, questioning, and rejection. As a result, the enemy would creep in with a lie, and I would listen. The more I pondered the lie, the more upset and angry I became.

I mentioned this to my aunt, because I wanted to be free of the anger and bitterness.

She suggested this: If I put my husband in God's pocket, then God had full control of him. At times, I would take my husband out of God's pocket, strangle him, and then put him back.

Why? I was hurting....

The visual of putting my husband in God's pocket helped me tremendously! As a wife, I had thought I had every right to tell God how to fix my husband. After all, he was not what I thought he should be. I went into marriage with a mixed-up concept of how a marriage should be—a fairy tale of a couple made up of Cinderella and Prince Charming.

My own parents, grandparents, family, church family, and friends all contributed to my concepts of a marriage. I took from them what I thought to be good and important truths. Putting those concepts into actual use is often difficult, as the spouse may or may not agree. In my case, my husband may not have seen things as I did, and possibly the issue was not as important to him.

When any person is hurting or disturbing you, put that person in God's pocket. Then you can work on yourself with the Holy Spirit's wisdom and guidance.

Going through this season has helped me focus on the Lord and give Him full reign and control of my life. I found that I had more free time on my hands, being without my husband and children, so I ventured into new and different ways to serve the Lord.

I miss my family! And would like to see our relationship restored. For now, I will continue serving the Lord as a single gal.

Does the idea of putting someone in God's pocket make sense to you?

PUT ALL YOUR CARE ON GOD

WHY?

BECAUSE

HE

CARES

FOR

YOU!

Mourning into Dancing

DANCING

Dancing, it is a choice!

You need to decide that you have had enough of the mourning, sackcloth, sorrow, and sadness. Sometimes you may not even know you have stepped out of the mourning and ashes...it just happens. Dancing — rejoicing.

You have moved past the "but why, God?" stage or season to this:

I have made up my mind I am going to rejoice and give thanks in ALL things, whether I understand or not!

Have you ever noticed that when you are happy, chipper, bouncy with enthusiasm and excitement; those things have a different light and look to them? The picture might be the same as yesterday, but your perspective has changed.

Look through God's heavenly, untainted lens. If you look at an image through a blurred lens you have a blurred view, right?

When the lens is clear and unobstructed, you see clearly.

Which lens are you looking through?

It does not matter what season you are in or at what stage in the circumstance that you are dealing with...

notes Ideas THOUGHTS

YOU ARE ABLE TO

REJOICE

AND

GIVE GOD THANKS

Mourning into Dancing

KEEP FOCUSSED

It is very easy to get distracted. We need to stay *focused* on Jesus.

Hebrews 12:1, 2
Therefore we also, since we are surrounded by so great a
*   cloud of witnesses, let us lay aside every weight, and the*
*   sin which so easily ensnares us, and let us run with*
*   endurance the race that is set before us,"*
:2 looking unto Jesus, the author and finisher of our faith, who
*   for the joy that was set before Him endured the cross,*
*   despising the shame, and has sat down at the right hand*
*   of the throne of God.*

Mourning into Dancing

At times, I have found it very hard to stay focused on the Lord. At the beginning of my separation, it seemed that everything was heavy and pressing down on me. It was as if I was trying to swim upstream. I was still in a state of shock, and my brain could not or would not comprehend this separation. There was a lot that needed to be addressed. I felt quite mixed up, as though I was jumping from one thing to another. I needed answers.

I praise God for strategically placing people in my path who had answers. At one workshop I attended, the instructor gave me information about legal aid, after he talked to his son, a lawyer. A counsellor gave me support ideas. The library had a room full of resources. I realized that people, even strangers, were quite willing to help. One evening after a legal workshop, I was about to go on the train, and was chatting with a lady who encouraged me and basically told me to keep my chin up. Many days it seemed I barely could move one foot forward, even a baby step and other days were better, and I accomplished more.

When I stayed focused on our Heavenly Father, things were not so daunting. Most situations were new to me: finding a new place to live by myself, budgeting, using the transit and LRT, relearning to drive a standard, working with the legal system, and going back to college after *many* years!

One-day God was speaking to me about staying close to Him, as He is the only one that can completely satisfy me.

He spoke this to me:

" Stay in the water...Stay in Me—dwelling, nourishing, drinking, enjoying ME.

Seek Me first. Stay focussed on me only.

I am your lover.

There is a time for everything. Allow Me to lead and guide you. I will make your way perfect. I will establish you...only I...

No man can do this! Seek Me first.

Matthew 6:25,26
Therefore I say to you, do not worry about your life, what you
will eat or what you will drink; nor about your body, what

*you will put on. Is not life more than food and the body
more than clothing?*

*:26 Look at the birds of the air, for they neither sow nor reap
nor gather into barns; yet your heavenly Father feeds
them. Are you not of more value than they?*

One day, God spoke to me about this scripture.

H<small>E SAID</small>,

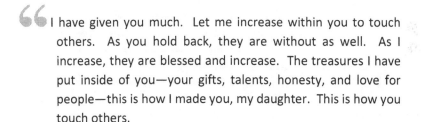I have given you much. Let me increase within you to touch
others. As you hold back, they are without as well. As I
increase, they are blessed and increase. The treasures I have
put inside of you—your gifts, talents, honesty, and love for
people—this is how I made you, my daughter. This is how you
touch others.

NOTES   Ideas   THOUGHTS

WILL YOU FOCUS?

ARE YOU FOCUSSING?

CAN YOU STAY FOCUSSED?

Mourning into Dancing

MIRY CLAY

God will help you out of the mud.

WHAT IS THE "MUD" in your life?

Could it be the areas that we are hanging onto? The things that hinder us from completely focusing on God? The gray areas that we totally do not talk about honestly?

To help understand the concept of miry clay:

MIRE — *swampy ground, mud.*

Psalm 69:1–3, 14
Save me, O God! For the waters have come up to my neck.
:2 I sink in deep mire, where there is no standing; I have come
    into deep waters, where the floods overflow me.

:3 I am weary with my crying; my throat is dry; my eyes fail while I wait for my God.

:14 Deliver me out of the mire, and let me not sink; let me be delivered from those that hate me, and out of the deep waters.

Pɪᴛ — *horrible pit of commotion and destruction*

Psalm 40:1–3

I waited patiently for the LORD; and He inclined to me, and heard my cry.

:2 He also brought me up out of a horrible pit, out of the miry clay, and set my feet upon a rock, and established my steps.

:3 He has put a new song in my mouth—praise to our God; many will see it and fear, and will trust in the LORD.

WHEN YOU FIND YOURSELF IN A HORRIBLE PIT...OR STUCK IN THE MIRY CLAY

Which actions best describe you?

Despair	Prayer
• cry	• call out for help
• whine	• pray
• become angry	• sing, worship and praise
• become frustrated	• thank God in all things
• give up hope	• persist
• lie back and die	• figure out ways to get out
• unclear vision	• stay focussed

What do you do? What is your immediate reaction?
Despair or Prayer?

Mourning into Dancing

When I talk about mud, I see myself covered in mud — sin and shame. Before I asked Jesus to enter my heart, I was covered in mud. I was a child of six, knowing I had done things that Father God was not pleased with. I needed a bath — a cleansing from the inside out.

I have come to realize that the mud does not bother our Heavenly Father. In loving me, He will get dirty with my mud, but He will not sin. That is why in the Gospels, we see Jesus talking to the adulteress, to tax collectors, to the rich and the poor.

There were times during this separation from my family that I could not move my feet, and I felt that I was sinking deeper and deeper. I felt despair, heartache, and devastation with no end in sight. Trying to describe the enormity of all I felt and was going through is very overwhelming. Major decisions pressed down on me, daily tasks often were unbearable, breathing was hard to do...so I would walk and walk and walk. This was good medicine and therapy...

...BUT *PRAYER* ultimately is the best medicine.

NOTES **Ideas** **THOUGHTS**

DESPAIR

OR

PRAYER

Mourning into Dancing

MARRIAGE VOWS

*M*ourning and Death.

- Mourning: *grieving, sorrow.*
- Death is final, and you live with unanswered questions.

THIS WORD IS USUALLY RELATED to death of a person. We miss the person. We are at a loss without that person.

So many times, during the first and second years of my separation, I wished my husband had died.

It sounds terrible, but the reality was that I could handle the finality of death more than wondering how this separation happened and dealing with the unanswered questions of *why?*

ON OUR WEDDING Day many years ago, we vowed:

- *in sickness and in*
- *health. for richer or poorer.*

- *till death do us part.*

79

Mourning into Dancing

This was a vow. What is a vow?

• *a promise, bond, pledge, oath, commitment*

It was broken by lies, hurt, pain, and anger. There was no energy to push through, because of the stress and turmoil.

In a separation/divorce, your questions may never be answered. But one thing I learned was to not keep insisting on having my questions answered. The more I desired and longed to know the answers, the more I dwelt on that desire. It drove me.

Finally, a friend stopped me in my tracks. She spoke very wise words, so please take heed:

* What if you get the answer to the question and it messes you up even more than before?
* What if you are not prepared for the answer?
* Would it not be better to not know than to then need to deal with the answer?

I agreed with my friend. I backed off and let go of the urgency and desire to know the answer. Also, I gave that problem to God to carry for me.

If your spouse has betrayed you by having an affair, or been unfaithful, I am sure that you have many unanswered questions. I know for myself, that many questions and wonderings went through my head. I have no idea if my spouse was unfaithful, but there were a few times when I wondered. I do know that the enemy plays havoc on our minds during these moments of rejection and hurt.

I am very grateful for the wisdom of others.

I asked a pastor friend to share his thoughts on the marriage vow:

" In 1999, World Wide Pictures produced a movie, *A Vow to Cherish*. The title says it all. The marriage vow is supposed to be cherished. In life, we find ourselves making commitments to a lot of things: work, friends, school, church, and the list goes on.

Yet there is only ONE commitment that we make in the following words: "This ring I give to you as a reminder of my love. And I pledge my loyalty and devotion to you until we are separated by death."

This kind of a vow should be cherished. We are able to keep this vow (life commitment) only if we cherish it so much that we are willing to change in order to preserve it.

UCLA psychologists Thomas Bradbury and Benjamin Karney in their research with 172 couples over a period of eleven years came to the following conclusion: Couples in which both individuals were willing to make sacrifices for the sake of the marriage were significantly more likely to have more lasting and happy marriages.

— PASTOR SIMON

•

What are your thoughts and thinking about this subject, the marriage vow?

Do you agree with the research that took place with the 172 couples?

How can you or I emphasize the importance of the marriage vow?

NOTES Ideas THOUGHTS

Mourning into Dancing

STRIVING

Strive

- *to struggle in opposition to another*
- *to be in contention or dispute*
- *to make great efforts to achieve or obtain something*

OFTEN, God tells me to *stop struggling and stop striving.* The expression "let go and let God" is so true!

I need to let go of me and my ideas and let the Holy Spirit flow in and through me.

Once I do, I have peace and can *trust* God, and then I can see from His perspective and through His eyes.

There is one area in which striving is positive: we can desire to live our best for God and strive to do this. I see, even in this, that as my mother says, "when we keep focused on Jesus" or "Fix our eyes on Jesus," then everything will fall into place. We do not have to strive to do our best. We will naturally be doing our best, naturally in the spirit.

NOTES   Ideas   THOUGHTS

LET GO

AND

LET GOD

Mourning into Dancing

EACH STEP I TAKE

We have been wounded; physically, emotionally, mentally, spiritually...

Now it is time to take small steps forward.

It is important to allow yourself time to *grieve*. This will help you heal.

Sometimes it may seem that you have been at one phase or stage forever. Do not lose heart. Do not give in or give up.

YOU ARE NOT ALONE — NEVER EVER!

Joshua 1:5-7b

:5 No man shall be able to stand before you all the days of
your life; as I was with Moses, so I will be with you. I will
not leave you nor forsake you.

:6 Be strong and of good courage, for to this people you shall
divide as an inheritance the land which I swore to their
fathers to give them.

:7b Only be strong and very courageous...

Hebrews 13:5

:5 Let your conduct be without covetousness; be content with
such things as you have. For He Himself has said, "I will
never leave your nor forsake you."

At this stage that you are currently at, what type of steps are
you taking?

-baby
-inch by inch
-giant
-confident
-important
-casual
-no idea

EACH STEP

I TAKE,

GOD

GOES WITH ME

NOTES   Ideas   THOUGHTS

Mourning into Dancing

Mourning into Dancing

UNDER CONSTRUCTION

Father God
will *never* leave you or *forsake you.*
Yes, my world has just been turned *upside down.*

I am broken, bruised, and injured. My world has just fallen apart.

WHO AM I NOW? There is turmoil, confusion, despair, questions, hurt, pain, agony, numbness, anger, bitterness, anguish, rejection, accusation, fear, doubt, lies...to name just a few. When you are under construction there is need of repair, healing, restoration, rest, and health.

> *Ephesians 2:10*
> *For we are His workmanship, created in Christ Jesus for good*
> *works, which God prepared beforehand that we should*
> *walk in them.*
> *Psalm 100:3*

Know that the LORD, He is God; it is He who has made us, and
not we ourselves; we are His people and the sheep of His
pasture.

RECONSTRUCTION

Reconstruction must occur from the *inside out!* And it must start with my heart. It is a time of reprogramming my thinking from negative to positive, but it is also so much more. I have been encouraged and blessed by knowing that I am God's handiwork or workmanship.

Just because my husband rejected me and dumped me, does not mean my Heavenly Father will. He has created me with a plan and purpose and loves me through thick and thin. He is faithful to His promises and will never leave me.

Heavenly Father is the miracle-working God, and His desire is to transform me from a dirty, ugly vessel to a vessel of gold and worth, or as 2 Timothy 2:20, 21 says:

> *:20 But in a great house there are not only vessels of gold and*
> *silver, but also of wood and clay, some for honor and some*
> *for dishonor.*
> *:21 Therefore if anyone cleanses himself from the latter, he*
> *will be a vessel for honor, sanctified and useful for the*
> *Master, prepared for every good work.*

I may be bruised and broken, but I know that my Father God cherishes me and loves me even though I have flaws. This is beyond my comprehension. He is so patient and loving as He draws me back to Him, after I have sat in the mud of my sin and brokenness.

Sometimes I remained stuck because I did not know that I was stuck in a rut—or it may have been that I stubbornly chose to do so.

Life hands us situations and circumstances. We choose how we are going to deal with them. As I have journeyed on this path, I have had to choose wisely. Many times, I just prayed, because I had no idea what to do. Sometimes I just jumped in with both feet and plunged myself into a mess.

Father God was with me all the way, never scolding and always patient. Heavenly Father uses my mistakes for my good, and I can say that I do learn from them.

HEALING AND RESTORING - A TIME TO UPROOT.

When there is a dandelion in my garden. I cannot just pull the flower and hope to eliminate the whole dandelion. There are deep roots involved with this dandelion.

I must dig around the stem and then go deeper, deeper to reach the roots. Then after a time, I can uproot this one dandelion. At times, the one area may have to wait, as other areas that are intertwined with the first needs to be dealt with. For example: the dandelion has long roots, but there may be a carrot growing in the same garden patch, and its roots are intertwined with the dandelion root.

Similarly, God will slowly start exposing things concerning my life. As I give Him full control over every area, He can start the uprooting process. An example of this is the anger issues that I had. My husband had told me at one time to either get help or leave. The anger was exposed. I went to a Christian psychologist and together we worked at some of the "w's" (what, where, when, why, and how).

This was an uprooting time, a time of digging and dealing with issues concerning anger. During this process, other things were brought out in the open. It was very hard to go through this, because I was needing to go back to childhood experiences and memories. Just like the carrot and dandelion, many areas were intertwined. Six weeks of sessions and I was on the road to healing more.

God will start to deal with things, and then He will gently dig around the area a little here and a little there. One day He will have dug enough away that the area is free to be uprooted. And after it is uprooted, He doesn't leave me hanging with an empty hole. He then fills the hole with Himself...fruits of the Spirit...His character, and He continues the slow process of healing and restoring. Because I was so used to the old way...old way of thinking, feeling, I must ask myself: am I ready for this new area?

97

It is difficult to reprogram and start fresh. The Holy Spirit reminds me that He is always with me, and I do not walk alone.

In reconstruction we remember that we are created in His image and are renewed by His Spirit. We need to desire to linger with Him. To renew our mind, we must pray and devour God's Word, which is His truth to us.

2 Corinthians 4:16
Therefore we do not lose heart. Even though our outward man is perishing, yet the inward man is being renewed day by day.

Our inner man is *renewed and revived* day by day.

CONSTRUCTION

&

RECONSTRUCTION

HEALING

&

RESTORATION

NOTES Ideas THOUGHTS

TRUST WITHOUT BORDERS

What is a border? *It is a dividing line, a boundary with no limits and no hindrance — a separating line.*

SINCE I WAS A YOUNG CHILD, I have had a relationship with my Heavenly Father. I recall people commenting on how I talked to God so easily and so naturally. I address Him as if He is present...and, well, He is.

My communication with God is good. After all, one does not need to use proper and distinguished wording.

I *trust* my Heavenly Father. Yes, there are many times when I half-heartedly trust because I am afraid or wary.

Gentle Father helps me and leads me through. Sometimes He speaks strongly to get my attention, because I am not listening.

When my marriage began to fall apart, I leaned increasingly on Father God. He is my husband, my father, the Lord of lords, and the great I Am.

To *trust God without borders* for me means: to trust unconditionally, let it all go, and *let God, and t*o totally surrender to Him without voicing my opinion or ideas.

He knows my path. He goes before me and with me. I am not on some abstract trail, going who knows where. At times, it has felt like that: I have no idea how I got where I was. No idea why my marriage fell apart. No idea how to fix it. No idea how to even navigate from A to B.

I learned to let go and allow God to be the pilot. It is hard to let go of the controls. It is hard to not have control. Very hard. It can make you feel like a puppet with no control over anything.

As I *allow* God to move and pilot me, I become free, and I learn to dance without hindrance.

TO OBEY IS BETTER THAN TO SACRIFICE

Obey: *submit to, yield to*
Sacrifice: *give something up, surrender for the sake of getting something.*

> 1 Samuel 15:22
> So Samuel said: "Has the LORD as great delight in burnt
>   offerings and sacrifices, as in obeying the voice of the LORD?
>   Behold, to obey is better than sacrifice, and to heed than the
>   fat or rams."

As we yield to God our life, we are giving Him the greatest sacrifice that we can give. If we cannot give Him all, then who do we think we are? He is the potter and we are just mere clay in His hands. We are just flesh, and blood and He is God Almighty.

God knows your longings, desires, needs. After all, He made you! Don't you think He can care for you? He knows how many hairs you have on your head. Do not sacrifice yourself or shortchange yourself. It is not worth it. It will always equal regret.

Take time to heal. Take time to find out who God is—your healer, creator, master, savior, the great I Am. Take this time before pursuing another spouse, because if you have not allowed God to heal you, another spouse will hinder your healing journey.

A lot of people jump from relationship to relationship, or marriage to marriage, without doing a self-checkup.

Think of having a car. For it to run properly, you must have maintenance done. Doing a self-checkup allows you a chance to breathe and inspect yourself for damage or to inspect and ask yourself questions like: how did I end up here, or how can I avoid a situation like this in the future?

sacrifice = *mourning, regret*
obedience = *dancing, rejoicing*

I created this picture to illustrate leaving the old baggage behind and exchanging it for all that God has offered me.

Have you found yourself carrying a lot of unnecessary baggage? Does this baggage bother and burden you? There is a simple solution. Reach out to Jesus. Call out to Jesus. Cry out to Jesus. He is ready to lift the weight off you and give you freedom and hope.

Can you name other forms of baggage that have weighed you down? Write down the wonderful attributes that Jesus provides and gives you in exchange.

CAN YOU TRUST GOD WITH

YOUR LIFE?

CAN YOU TRUST GOD WITH NO DOUBTS OR QUESTIONS?

NOTES   Ideas   THOUGHTS

Mourning into Dancing

FINDING MY WORTH

As a wife of a husband and a mother of four children, I had many titles: wife, mom, cook, housekeeper, taxi driver, teacher, nurse, shopper, and the list continue.

I often was lost in all those titles and activities associated with them, with no idea who *I was or where* I had lost myself along the way.

At the beginning of my separation, I was quite lost. First, my husband was gone, and second, my children were not there. I was a single gal again, living by myself in a new place. This was quite unnerving. I was dealing with a woman I did not really know in a strange and new environment, dealing with things I had never dreamt of.

It has taken me a while to find out *who* I am. In various ways, God has shown to me **who** I am in Him and **how** He sees me: through His Word, through books, through Sunday church messages, and through people speaking the truth of who I am.

I was looked upon as "so and so's daughter," "so and so's wife," and "so and so's mother." Then I was slammed up against a wall, and everything changed. People did not know what to call me and would shy away. I also did not know how to respond to the new titles assigned to me.

107

THANKFULLY, GOD KNEW WHO I WAS!

Psalm 139:17,18
:17 How precious also are Your thoughts to me, O God! How
great is the sum of them!
:18 If I should count them, they would be more in number than
the sand; when I awake, I am still with You.

Isaiah 54:5
For your Maker is your husband, the LORD of hosts is His
name; and your Redeemer is the Holy One of Israel; He is
called the God of the whole earth.

Isaiah 49:16
See, I have inscribed you on the palms of My hands; your walls
are continually before Me.

Isaiah 62:1-12, refers to the restoration of Zion. I like to insert my name in the passage, so it reads: "*...the restoration of Wanda.*" You can insert your name here and in the following verses...

:1 For Zion's sake I will not hold My peace, and for
Jerusalem's sake I will not rest, until her righteousness goes
forth as brightness, and her salvation as a lamp that burns.
:2 The Gentiles shall see your righteousness, and all kings your
glory. you shall be called by a new name, which the mouth
of the LORD will name.
:3 You shall also be a crown of glory in the hand of the LORD,
and a royal diadem in the hand of your God.
:4 You shall no longer be termed Forsaken, nor shall your land
any more be termed Desolate; but you shall be called
Hephzibah, and your land Beulah; for the LORD delights in
you, and your land shall be married.

Ezekiel 36:33-36, is referring to the cleansing of the land.

I like to insert my name in the passage, so it reads: *"On the day that I cleanse Wanda from all her iniquities..."* You can insert your name here and in the following verses.

> *:33 Thus says the Lord GOD: "On the day that I cleanse you*
> *from all your iniquities, I will also enable you to dwell in*
> *the cities, and the ruins shall be rebuilt."*
> *:34 The desolate land shall be tilled instead of lying desolate in*
> *the sight of all who pass by.*
> *:35 So they will say, 'This land that was desolate has become*
> *like the garden of Eden; and the wasted, desolate, and*
> *ruined cities are now fortified and inhabited."*
> *:36 Then the nations which are left all around you shall know*
> *that I, the LORD, have rebuilt the ruined places and*
> *planted what was desolate. I, the LORD, have spoken it,*
> *and I will do it.*

These verses have become true in my life. At times, I had wondered if the wounds and scars would ever heal. And yes, a lot have. I had to allow the Holy Spirit to take control.

I AM BEGINNING TO DANCE!

> *Genesis 50:20*
> *But as for you, you meant evil against me; but God meant it*
> *for good, in order to bring it about as it is this day, to save*
> *many people alive.*

In this verse, Joseph is speaking to his brothers after they sold him into slavery and then came to Egypt looking for food.

I know that the enemy has tried to destroy me, but he is not winning! Every tactic and plan of the enemy is "going down." My Heavenly Father is all-knowing, all-powerful; He is Father God in heaven, the Redeemer of my soul, the One and Only who loves me unconditionally.

He has all power and authority to do what He wants in my life. He has transformed me and recreated me in His image. I am a work in process. I am His delight, the delight of the Holy One, the Mighty One.

He loves me so much that angels of the Lord are encamped around me

MOURNING INTO DANCING

He has turned my mourning into dancing. He has put off my sackcloth. He has girded me with gladness.

I WILL SPEAK up about what God has done and is doing in my life.

THANKFULLY, GOD KNOWS WHO WE ARE!

NOTES   Ideas   THOUGHTS

GOD'S PROMISES

The book of Psalms is loaded with God's promises.

MANY TIMES, when I needed reassurance, encouragement, godly wisdom, or something else, God leads me to the Psalms.

    5: A morning prayer
    18: God's help in distress
    27: Confidence in God
    33: God's provision
    37: Instruction
    46: The presence of God in calamity
    51: Truth and cleansing
    91: Security of the godly
    118: The Lord's mercy
    147: The Lord's Grace

I ENCOURAGE you to read the Psalms, which contain a vast array of God's promises.

What chapters and verses in the PSALMS have ministered to you?

NOTES Ideas THOUGHTS

GOD'S PROMISES

SHAKE OFF YOUR SLUMBER

To "shake off" means to *throw off or get rid of.*

Isaiah 30:22
You will also defile the covering of your images of silver, and the ornament of your molded images of gold. You will

throw them away as an unclean thing; you will say to them, "get away!"

DEFILE—*BREAK in pieces, throw down, destroy*

WHAT IS AN IDOL?

Anything that takes time away from our God, including time, money, friends, and activities.

I believe that mourning and grief have their place. For myself, there have been times when I get hit with things I have not thought of for a long time. I realize that the enemy does not like that I have healed and moved on. I may still have moments of loneliness, but I am not alone. I may have a fleeting thought of companionship, a desire for it, but these thoughts pass. If I do not linger on the thought, it passes like a leaf floating freely down in the breeze...flittering and fluttering aimlessly down, down, down.

Sometimes this is easier to type on a piece of paper than to do. Once again, I want to say that *yes,* if we both have changed, I would like my husband back. But in the meantime, I will linger in God's presence and seek Him to bring comfort and peace.

I encourage you, dear friend, to find yourself in your heavenly Father before pursuing a relationship.

May you not have "idols" in your life. May you be free of the shackles and chains that bind and try to corrupt and obstruct your life. Seek peace, but most importantly, *"seek you first the kingdom of God."*

God does not see me as broken; He sees me as whole.

I AM DANCING!

I need to get past the worldly way of thinking and see myself as *whole*. Then I literally need to put into practice the way that I walk... think... speak... act.

The worldly way of thinking is not bad in some respects, but the world does not have Jesus, who is our source of life.

Father God once said to me,

> "*Have complete trust in Me*! I hold your hand. I am walking with you. I am for you. I have so much more for you. Seek me first! Be still and wait for Me, only Me. I satisfy you. Be lost in Me. Let it all go, and be lost in Me."

It is like riding a bicycle on a country road. You approach a hill with no idea what the other side of the hill looks like. You are trusting, so ready and eager to pedal up and down the other side.

The wind is blowing in your hair. The sun is warm on your skin. You have energy to push and pump your legs—up, down, up, down—flying, floating, free, and carefree.

It is so thrilling, enthralling, relaxing...so enjoyable.

I HAVE TURNED YOUR MOURNING INTO DANCING.
DANCE WITH ME!

NOTES   Ideas   THOUGHTS

F

O

R

G

I

V

E

N

AND

FREE

Mourning into Dancing

VENGEANCE AND JUDGING

If you truly desire to be finished with the season of mourning and you are so ready for the season of dancing,
then *shake off* the desire and urge for vengeance.

VINDICTIVENESS—*HAVING an unrealistic desire for revenge*

> *Hebrews 10:30*
> *For we know Him who said, "Vengeance is Mine, I will repay,"*
> *says the Lord. And again, "The LORD will judge His people."*

> *Romans 12:19*
> *Beloved, do not avenge yourselves, but rather give place to*
> *wrath; for it is written, "Vengeance is Mine, I will repay,"*
> *says the Lord.*

This is a very tough thing to act upon. It is easier to talk about it. I know that I initially wanted my spouse to experience everything I was suffering. I thought he had to, for me to feel better. I wanted payback.

I was hurting, so he needed to hurt, as well. My pennies were being pinched, so I wanted his pinched too.

If we allow vengeance to eat at us, we become even more angry and bitter. We will be full of hatred instead of *joy.*

> *Joshua 24:15*
> *And if it seems evil to you to serve the LORD, choose for*
> *yourselves this day whom you will serve, whether the gods*
> *which your fathers served that were on the other side of the*
> *river, or the gods of the Amorites, in whose land you dwell.*
> *But as for me and my house, we will serve the LORD.*

Let go of the wrong and unfairness that have been dealt to you. Leave everything to God; He can deal with it.

When we let go of the vengeance, we set ourselves free.

Free — free from the weight, free to move on, free to pursue life and not death.

THOUGHTS FROM A FRIEND,

 Vengeance: gives temporary relief from our pain. Then the guilt sets in and we must deal with that.

Think before you act. Just because we want others to have pain or suffer like we have does not mean they will.

We need to run from it. Vengeance is for the Lord; we need to let Him deal with it."

— PAMELA

FREE

TO

DANCE!

NOTES   Ideas   THOUGHTS

Mourning into Dancing

Mourning into Dancing

GREAT IS YOUR FAITHFULNESS

He is such a faithful Father. His love knows no end. His peace passes all understanding, and He is so good to me. I love when I see God in a beautiful display of clouds and color in a sunset or sunrise. Or in the geese on the river. Or in a raindrop on an Albertan rose out on a trail. Or in the smell of a spruce or pine tree on an early-morning walk— so fragrant.

One day I was worshipping the Lord during a prayer time with my church. I was not asking Him for anything. I just wanted to adore Him, and He showed me a picture. I love spruce and pine trees, and God knows this. We were out walking and enjoying one another.

He overwhelms me with His love, presence, goodness, peace, patience, and faithfulness.

His patience for me is overwhelming! And He loves me continuously, no matter how many times I get sidetracked by this and that or make the same mistake over and over.

I always feel so safe and secure, so loved on these walks that God and I take.

Can you think about how God has been a faithful Father to you?
How has He revealed Himself to you as a Father?

FAITHFUL

FATHER

NOTES   Ideas   THOUGHTS

FORGIVENESS

Let go of the past. You cannot change the past, but you can change the present. You cannot undo the past, but you can forgive.

THERE ARE two very important aspects of forgiveness: one is to forgive yourself, and the second is to forgive the other person, whether that person accepts your forgiveness. Through forgiving, you have done your part and can now move on and be free.

I have found that it is very difficult to forgive myself. I believe I still am forgiving, and it is a process that takes time. With each memory that comes to me, I must release it back to God to carry.

Thankfully, Jesus's death on the cross and my entreaty to Him to come live in my heart—my desire to become His child—have given me access to be free from the burden of the hurts and pain.

Forgiveness can be a tough task to deal with. Do you want to move on? Then you must forgive. Ask Father God to help you forgive those who have hurt you during your separation/divorce. I know that He has helped me forgive my spouse. Forgiveness is an experience that has freed me

...and now I can dance!

NOTES   Ideas   THOUGHTS

TO

FORGIVE

AND

TO

BE

FORGIVEN

THOUGHTS FROM FAMILY AND FRIENDS

Thoughts from Family and Friends...

"I'm Not in Love with You Anymore," by **Jenny** (family, divorced)

❝Jenny, I'm not in love with you anymore. I love you like I love my mom and sister." These are words no wife wants to hear from her husband, the man she committed to for the rest of her life. It took me months to process what was going to be my new reality. My marriage had reached its breaking point and was coming to an end. There's no instruction manual on how to heal your heart when it's been shattered. I made the move from British Columbia back to Alberta, because in my heart that was always where my home was.

The day I was to move back, I felt all alone in beautiful British Columbia, packing up the last of my belongings and getting ready to leave the home I had shared with my husband. This was the start of a new chapter in my life, one of new beginnings and many fresh starts. My close friend Esther helped me get a job with the federal government in Edmonton, where she worked. I was so happy to be moving back to my true home of Alberta. I had to say good-bye to Jackson, the dog my husband and I shared. I will never forget the sadness in Jackson's face when I left that evening. I felt so sad, knowing I had tried so very hard to save my marriage. I had thought I could love enough for the both of us and make the marriage work.

I read the book *The Love Dare* by Alex Kendrick and Stephen Kendrick, which inspired the movie *Fireproof*. I was hoping for a miracle for my marriage, and the movie and book gave me lots of hope. Also, I had a few close friends who were having troubles in their marriages, and over time they reconciled. I thought they had far worse issues in their marriages than I did. I was waiting for a miracle that never came.

One day, with a lot of courage, I let go of all hope that I could reconcile with my former husband, and a huge weight was lifted off me. God told me, "Jenny, if you want to be happy, the choice is up to you."

Since I moved back to Alberta, I've never had to worry about money, and God has always provided me with good jobs. Even to this day God is looking out for me financially. God has blessed me with a wonderful family. I look at my life now and all I've accomplished on my own since my divorce—buying a home, buying a vehicle for the first time, building a good career in administration, and becoming an inspiration to other women and friends. But most importantly, I've become a stronger woman and much more independent than I ever was in my entire life. I proved to myself and everyone else I can stand tall despite my hardships. I'm proud of the woman I am today."

DEANNA (FRIEND FROM CHILDHOOD, divorced, married.)

<header>

</header>

Mourning into Dancing

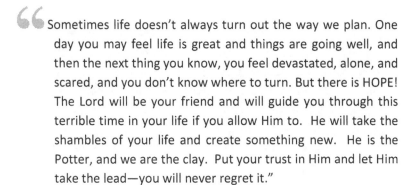 Sometimes life doesn't always turn out the way we plan. One day you may feel life is great and things are going well, and then the next thing you know, you feel devastated, alone, and scared, and you don't know where to turn. But there is HOPE! The Lord will be your friend and will guide you through this terrible time in your life if you allow Him to. He will take the shambles of your life and create something new. He is the Potter, and we are the clay. Put your trust in Him and let Him take the lead—you will never regret it."

Karol (my mother, married over thirty-seven years and widowed twenty years)

My Daughter

 "...that our daughters may be as [corner] pillars, sculptured in palace style..." Psalm 144:12b (NKJV)

"...that our daughters may be as corner stones, polished after the similitude of a palace..." Psalm 144:12b (KJV)

When Wanda was six or so, my mom sent this verse in a letter. The Lord showed me that this is how God saw Wanda. I believed, and still believe, that God has been "sculpturing" Wanda into a beautiful "pillar" in His Kingdom.

As I watched Wanda during her growing-up years, I saw a girl, a teenager who had such a giving heart, always reaching out to others. Wanda asked Jesus into her heart when she was six, was filled with the Holy Spirit when she was eight, and was baptized in water when she was ten. She had a heart call to Africa and its people when she was twelve. She still loves the African people.

Wanda met her husband in 1988; they married in 1989. They worked tirelessly for the Lord, in an international missionary work, for ten years, in California and British Columbia. Then moved to Alberta with their four children.

After many years of circumstances and situations, their relationship declined, and their marriage ended. Wanda was told to leave and start life somewhere else on her own. After Wanda had lived with relatives for a month, God helped her find a wee little basement suite, partially furnished.

From that small beginning, I have seen the Lord provide for her, over and over.

But more than being provided material provisions, I have watched Wanda during this severe "sculpturing/polishing" time in her life. As hard as it has been for her, I have watched as she has developed a closer relationship with our Lord Jesus than she had ever experienced in her life. Truly, it has been a journey from... *Mourning to Dancing!*

Revelation 3:12 "...He [She] who overcomes, I will make him [her] a pillar in the temple of My God...."

~

JULIE (FRIEND I met at DivorceCare, separated eight years, mother of three)

❝ One of the biggest things I learned during all this is that God is sovereign. I knew it, but I never realized what that meant. It means that nothing happens to us that He doesn't allow. In the book of Job, chapter 1, we see Satan approaching God for permission to come against Job. Satan must ask God's permission! And God sets the parameters within which the devil must operate:

"everything he has is in your power, but on the man, himself do not lay a finger" (Job 1:12). That means that anything that comes against us has been orchestrated by God Himself for a good purpose, because He promises *"that all things work for the good of those who love Him" (Romans 8:28).*

When I finally put all of this together in my own life, it gave me such freedom from stress and anxiety. It's only been recently that I've begun to understand what His purpose is for all that I've been through, whether it was to teach me something, to draw me closer to Him, to use me to help others, or any other reason.

God is in control of my situation and is with me in my trials, and I can trust Him that He's doing what is best for me on an eternal scale, because He loves me."

~

TAMARA (COUSIN, single mom of one son, now married over sixteen years, grandmother of two)

When you feel absolute despair from the shame of your actions and you think that no one could ever love you because you don't love yourself—and even if you may be thinking of ending your life because that is what you
think you deserve— please do not believe or take these thoughts to heart for one moment! Such thoughts and feelings are lies from the enemy. God's truth is that His love IS for you and that you are never beyond His love, even if you think you can't be loveable because of the shameful things you have done. God's desire is for you to receive His love. He doesn't look at you the way you look at yourself. He sent his son to die on a cross to pay the price for your sins. Once you receive and take His love into your heart, and once you believe not just notionally (conceptually) that God loves you, and once you let go of the lies that your worth and value come from people's approval, you will go from feeling like the worst person to knowing that you are loved and valued beyond measure!"

~

JANE-GAL (A DEAR FRIEND FROM CHURCH, married and mother of two)

141

"God is a God of hope, and for every step He has a master plan for our lives. He does not reveal everything in a day. His desire is for us to walk with Him day by day, trusting Him to guide our paths. As human beings, we want to know our path right now, right here. That, however, is not depending on a loving and caring father.

As scripture says in *Jeremiah 1:5 of The Message:* "*Before I shaped you in the womb, I knew all about you. Before you saw the light of day, I had holy plans for you.*"

Psalm 139:13–16 continues, "*For you created my inmost being; you knit me together in my mother's womb. (14) I praise you because I am fearfully and wonderfully made; your works are wonderful, I know that full well. (15) My frame was not hidden from you when I was made in the secret place, when I was woven together in the depths of the earth. (16) Your eyes saw my unformed body; all the days ordained for me were written in your book before one of them came to be.*"

God knows each and every day even before it unfolds. He knows the words we say even before we think about what we want to say. Nothing comes to our lives without getting a stamp of approval from Him. He allows things to take place in our lives to make us and shape us into who He wants us to be. Our role is to continue to hope in His love, knowing that He holds everything in place and trusting His heart even when we do not see His hand moving in our lives. When we have hope, we can then walk day by day, taking one day at a time, knowing He is leading. We can follow in security, knowing all is well in Abba's hands.

I have watched as God transformed Wanda and molded her to get her where she is in her walk today. Wanda's life is a life full of hope, prayer, endurance, and victory. God has a lot more in store for Wanda in the future."

～

DAVINA (AUNT, married twenty-six years)

 A miracle: *a cocoon becomes a butterfly.*

Have you ever seen a beautiful, multicolored butterfly emerging from a cocoon? I did, not literally, but metaphorically. A few years ago, Wanda's life had turned 180 degrees, and the world around her was upside down. She had no idea what she was supposed to do and how she was to handle day-to-day-life without a familiar environment. She had experienced a lot of "FIRST-TIME" experiences, like using city transportation, renting a place to live, going back to school, learning to draw and pastel. Now, she has turned out to be a confident, self-reliant person; she is the beautiful woman that God intended her to be, inside and out! Most of all, her faith in God never fails her, and it becomes stronger every day."

PAMELA (DEAR FRIEND I met at DivorceCare, separated seven years, recently divorced, mother of three wonderful boys)

 The evening my husband left was one of the hardest days, yet it brought the biggest relief I have ever felt.

You see, I had been living a lie for more than twelve years. Yes, as a Christian woman, I was making bad choices and breaking the vows, I took in front of God and family. You see, I had been hiding my feelings from my husband for a very long time, for fear that I would be rejected and misunderstood. All I wanted was to be understood and heard and safe. This was not possible with him, and although I reached out more times than I can remember, I turned to other ways to cope.

I binge drank with close friends, and I had numerous affairs. I acted as if all was well and went to church every Sunday, but I hid what was really in my heart. My close friends knew the struggle, but I couldn't tell anyone else. I was ashamed of who I was, what I had done, and what I was doing. I felt worthless and suicidal, often dealing with depression and anxiety throughout all my marriage, yet I was happy, with so many things in my life, especially my three wonderful boys.

Fast-forward to after my separation; I never wanted so badly to live, to prove that I could be a good mother and be alive and do right by my boys. I wanted to raise my boys the way I knew I could and be a good role model and mother. I had no idea my husband would use every means possible to ruin every relationship I had, including that with our boys. He went to any length to expose my affairs, my spending, my messy house, and any other shred of evidence to get my family, church, and friends to turn against me. He hacked my e-mails and computer and did everything possible to prove I was unfit.

I would cry out to God to stop him—to stop the pain and stop the hurt I had so deep in my heart. One thing that I always thought was, I am not going to fight dirty. It was not right to fight back with evil. I would hold my head up and try and do right. For once in my life, I would do something right.

I had read so many books about divorce and parenting. All I really needed was the Bible and some help interpreting it for me, a child of God. I found some helpful books to help me understand God's love for me and His grace.

See, the hardest thing was forgiving myself. I still struggle to do this; however, every day I get stronger and let God's love surround me increasingly. In the past, I kept people from getting close because I didn't think anyone would love me if they knew the real me. Well, God loves me unconditionally. Nothing I do will make Him love me less, and nothing I did in my past makes Him love me less or more. I don't know what I would have done without this love.

God has sent me people to love me, help heal me, and guide me to Him. I do feel sometimes that I was punished by God in my dealings with judges and court and people. I know God had His hand in it, to teach me some hard lessons and help build me up to be the stronger woman I am today.

I am proud to say I did what I felt what was best for my kids at the time, and I didn't fight dirty. If I have done anything right in this life, one thing is that I tried my best to honor God in my divorce proceedings. God paved the way for me, and I will be faithful and trust Him in all situations. I trusted Him with my divorce, and He became more real than He ever had been in all my life. Praise be to God for His love and faithfulness."

NOTES   Ideas   THOUGHTS

Mourning into Dancing

UP FROM THE ASHES, IT IS A MIRACLE

When this book was almost finished, my divorce became finalized.

HERE ARE some verses and thoughts that God gave me.

GOD HAS LIFTED the weight of the divorce from me, and I am not drowning in the clutches of its despair and devastation. In the previous pages of this book, you read that I did not choose this path of separation and divorce. I still do not like that I am on this journey, and I am not jumping up and down in exhilaration. But I have determined that the enemy is not going to win! *"I can do all things through Christ, who strengthens me."* I will be joyful and positive. I know that Father God goes before me and that He has a plan and purpose for my life.

UP FROM THE ASHES...
A NEW BEGINNING...
A FRESH START...

How amazing that a plant will start to grow.

UP
FROM THE
ASHES OF A
DEVASTATING FIRE...

Isaiah 60:1,5b

:1 Arise, shine; for your light has come! And the glory of the LORD is risen upon you.

:5b Then you shall see and become radiant, and your heart shall swell with joy...

Isaiah 30:15a, 18,19

:15a For thus says the Lord GOD, the Holy One of Israel: "In returning and rest you shall be saved; in quietness and confidence shall be your strength..."

:18 Therefore the LORD will wait, that He may be gracious to you; And therefore He will be exalted, that He may have mercy on you. For the LORD is a God of justice; blessed are all those who wait for Him.

150

:19 For the people shall dwell in Zion at Jerusalem; you shall
weep no more. He will be very gracious to you at the
sound of your cry; when He hears it, He will answer you.

Thank you, Father, for what You have *instilled* in me. It is *You* in me. I am nothing without You!

How unsearchable are His thoughts?
How vast is the sum of them? How magnificent are His ways?
My heart explodes with the magnitude of His mercy and grace,
and He loves me! Who am I that He loves and cares for me?

Romans 11:33
Oh, the depth of the riches both of the wisdom and knowledge
of God! How unsearchable are His judgments and His
ways past finding out!
Lord, I look to You; where does my help come from?

Isaiah 61:3

*To console those who mourn in Zion, to give them beauty for
ashes, the oil of joy for mourning, the garment of praise for
the spirit of heaviness; that they may be called trees of
righteousness, the planting of the LORD, that He may be
glorified.*

Psalm 3:3
*But You, O LORD, are a shield for me, my glory and the One
who lifts up my head.*

Shield

- *When God is your shield, He surrounds you, and nothing can
touch your life unless He lets it.*
- *There is a God-ordained purpose for everything that happens
to you.*

Lifter Up of My Head

- *A person's head is normally bent down in time of trouble. He has
lifted our head, so it is not bent down.*
- *When we have bad news, we bend our head down — or if we are
mourning, we cover our head and bend it down.*
- *When we have good news, instantly our head rises, and we
"see the light of day" and rejoice.*

1 Peter 1:6-9
*:6 In this you greatly rejoice, though now for a little while, if
need be, you have been grieved by various trials,*
*:7 that the genuineness of your faith, being much more
precious than gold that perishes, though it is tested by fire,
may be found to praise, honor, and glory at the revelation
of Jesus Christ,*

:8 whom having not seen you love. Though now you do not
see Him, yet believing, you rejoice with joy inexpressible
and full of glory,
:9 receiving the end of your faith—the salvation of your souls.

1 Peter 5:6,7
:6 Therefore humble yourselves under the mighty hand of
God, that He may exalt you in due time,
:7 casting all your care upon Him, for He cares for you.

YOU ARE MY FATHER

Loving, glorious, caring, good, supporting, strong, cherishing, faithful, sustaining, true, kind, holy, just, pure, righteous.

Zephaniah 3:16,17
:16 In that day it shall be said to Jerusalem: "Do not fear; Zion,
let not your hands be weak.
:17 The LORD your God in your midst, The Mighty One, will
save; He will rejoice over you with gladness, He will quiet
you with His love, He will rejoice over you with singing.

With each victory that you achieve, the less of a hold the enemy will have on your life. Be aware of every distraction, disturbance, and discouragement.

GOD IS THE WINNER!

Genesis 18:14
Is anything too hard for the LORD? At the appointed time I will return to you, according to the time of life, and Sarah shall have a son.

Jeremiah 32:17, 27
:17 Ah, Lord GOD! Behold, You have made the heavens and
the earth by Your great power and outstretched arm.
There is nothing too hard for You.

:27 Behold, I am the LORD, the God of all flesh. Is there
anything too hard for Me?

Mark 10:27
But Jesus looked at them and said, "With men it is impossible,
but not with God; for with God all things are possible."

THERE IS NOTHING IMPOSSIBLE WITH GOD.

I am the one that limits Him from moving or flowing. My thoughts, whether good or bad, become a dam in the middle of the river. The flow is obstructed.

Release and surrender all your thoughts and ideas. Doing this then enables Father God to do His work.

Many things we go through may not have anything to do with us. God could possibly be using these things for someone else to benefit from or be blessed by.

I AM MAKING ALL THINGS NEW

Isaiah 43:18, 19
:18 Do not remember the former things, nor consider the
things of old.
:19 Behold, I will do a new thing, now it shall spring forth; Shall
you not know it? I will even make a road in the wilderness
and rivers in the desert.

Isaiah 41:18-20
:18 I will open rivers in desolate heights, and fountains in the
midst of the valleys; I will make the wilderness a pool of
water, and the dry land springs of water.
:19 I will plant in the wilderness the cedar and the acacia tree,
the myrtle and the oil tree; I will set in the desert the
cypress tree and the pine and the box tree together,

:20 That they may see and know, and consider and understand together, that the hand of the LORD has done this, and the Holy One of Israel has created it.

God's hands are protecting you as you submerge up from the ashes of separation and divorce.

New Song for a New Season
Are you ready to invest in a new song or new season?
Are you willing to have a fresh start? To begin again?

UP FROM THE ASHES, IT TRULY IS A MIRACLE.

NOTES   Ideas   THOUGHTS

MY FINAL THOUGHTS

As a child, if the thought had ever come to me that I would one day go through a divorce, I would have dismissed it and not believed it. There were few divorces back then and it was uncommon.

As tragic as a divorce is, there is life after it. Divorce can get ugly and devastating.

Now I have been married three years to a wonderful godly man. He is not perfect, and neither am I. God has blessed us with each other.

God is and has been faithful. God never changes. God never fails. And He always keeps His promises.

Life can be challenging and we must always watch our attitude, have a grateful heart, and praise God continually.

I have learned a lot in this second marriage.

I know that my life is a miracle.

Only God could take a gal from a muddy mirky situation, put her on solid ground, stablish her, and continue to show her what His plan for her is.

Only God can transform a life.

Only God can give meaning and purpose to life.

159

Only God can take the ugliness of a situation and turn it into something beautiful.

Only God can change shame and bitterness to peace and joy.

Only God can unconditionally love us through all situations and circumstances.

Only God will take a miserable nobody and make them into a wonderful somebody. A somebody that He loves and cherishes.

Only God can reveal and show us how to use our experiences to help, encourage and give hope to someone else.

Only God can turn the impossible to possible.

Only God can change a strong and determined mindset.

Only God can turn an unforgiving heart to forgiving and caring.

Only God can see our situation and disaster and give us wisdom and guidance to come out of it.

Only God can give strength and endurance in the middle of the storm.

Only God can take one from the ashes and give joy and peace.

Only God can give hope.

Only God

Over the years since writing the first edition of this book, I have talked to many people. Through our conversations, we realize that the happenings in our lives are similar, but different. Some people still are devastated and hurt by a divorce; others have sailed through. There are those, like myself, that have been blessed to remarry and continue with life and God's plan for them. Many divorced do not remarry. God definitely has a plan and purpose for their lives as well.

Personally, I am so grateful to God in bringing Larry into my life when He did. God orchestrated our marriage, partnership, and friendship.

Larry's motto in life is, "Go with the flow" and this has been the best medicine we can take. We live fulltime in our RV. My husband is semi-retired and I do not think that he has a "stop" button. He is always researching and figuring out better ways to do things and save money. I have learned a lot from him. I love that he includes me in decision making for our businesses and home. We have good communication.

We have been on many adventures. During our dating days, we both had a dream of writing and publishing books in a cabin by a lake. Living in our RV, our predictable destinations are in RV Parks, with access to swimming pools, where we do our workouts. We both have written many books in our home and we also manage our other businesses in the small space of our RV.

Early in our marriage we started the process to get my Green Card Status for the United States. Once we started this process, I was unable to return to Canada to visit family. (In that time a new grandbaby arrived and her older sister was growing up so quickly!) It took more than two years to finally get approved! (As of early summer 2021, the Canadian border is still locked down, due to Covid 19). One day I will visit my family and get to know my grandchildren!

We have met so many people in the many RV Parks in the United States that we have stayed at. Some are born again Christians and we have such good chats with them in the swimming pool and in our homes. Others are just ordinary people living life. There are many opportunities to share Jesus--not only in words, but in and through our daily lives.

My husband has golfed for many years and is coaching me. This is a sport that challenges me. I have some great swings and putts, and then I find myself searching for my ball in the bushes and water.

It reminds me of my journey throughout this life.

It is what I make of each situation. How do I handle myself? Am I getting frustrated and upset? Do I just "go with the flow," as my husband, Dr. Larry Robinson, so often suggests to me.

We are living in serious times in our world. There has been much upheaval and really, we have no idea what each day will bring. We do know who is in control and so there is no reason to worry. We can be smart and wise, but it is best to use God's wisdom and guidance in these days.

I am so very thankful for God's grace and mercy. His love and compassion-- to bless me with a new husband. Larry is different than my first husband, yet similar.

So, I still need to deal with me. Thought and attitude patterns are hard to get rid of or change, but it is possible. I need to persevere with God's endurance and strength. God has given Larry wisdom to help me through many of the things that have come up, or helped me see who I was battling. The enemy uses anything he can to bring turmoil, doubt, fear, stress, and more.

It is about wanting to change for the better.

Life does happen. I am older now and my thinking on life issues is different than it was even five years ago.

I need to accept today as now and continue in what God has shown me to do.

Occasionally, I have a flashback or a memory from my past. Do I linger on it beat myself up, or continue to experience the hurt and pain it had caused me? No! I need to realize where it is coming from. Is it just a thought or is it the enemy trying to mess me up? I then need to take the correct action and tell the enemy to *get lost in the Name of Jesus!* Or see it simply as a memory and then take the time to pray for the ones in the memory.

I must live in the now of life. I cannot change the past, but I can make today a good day with the choices and decisions I make. God has opened me up and poured in His goodness. I am truly blessed!

What is my purpose? Why do I write books? I have always been an encourager and this is my purpose to encourage the body of Christ.

I pray that this book, Mourning into Dancing: My Journey Through Separation and Divorce has encouraged you in some way.

Wanda Robinson

MY PRAYER FOR YOU

Father God, I lift each person who has read this book that You have given me to write. I thank You, Father, for giving us this opportunity to readjust ourselves and to possibly look at our situation through a different and clearer lens.

May all the readers experience Your freedom in their lives, and may they be able to walk in the newness of life that You freely give us.

Thank You, Father God, for always being there when we slip up, make mistakes, or get stuck in the mud.

I am so grateful for Your faithfulness!

Father, I ask that you continue to walk with each of us on our journey. In Your name, Amen.

ACKNOWLEDGMENTS

My deepest appreciation to my family and friends who prayed, encouraged, and supported me during the process of writing this book. Thank you is not enough, so I pray God's blessings over you.

I would also like to make special mention to you, family, and friends, who contributed a thought or insight into my book.

Pamela, Deanna, Julie, Tamara, Jenny, Karol (my mom), Davina (my aunt), Jane-gal, Preacher Rod Ngwenya, and Pastor Simon.

Special thanks to my husband Larry Robinson for his insight to update this book and for all his encouragement and ideas.

The following graphics designed by Freepik.com:

-free-vector/watercolor-butterflies-collectionmultipurpose_1182487--
-free-vector/collection-of-retro-glasses_804323
-free-vector/teamwork-concept-with-persons-holdingjigsaw-pieces_1832493
-free-vector/closeup-of-key-placed-on-vintagebible_1186587
-free-vector/happy-little-boy-in-motion-smiley-runningon-the-street_1025775
-free-vector/pink-watercolortexture_940298

ABOUT THE AUTHOR

Wanda Robinson enjoys golfing, swimming, crocheting, walks in God's creation, gardening, other people's cats and dogs, music from the "50's and 60's", and of course writing and creating books.

Wanda and her husband travel in their RV throughout the United States. Their desire is to follow God's leading and direction, and this finds them in many different places and with quite a variety of people. They also have a combined 6 children and 8 grandchildren. Wanda loves people of all ages and her desire is that people will come to know Jesus Christ's love, redemption, and hope for their lives. Wanda is originally from Alberta, Canada.

Wanda Robinson's books are available:

amazon.com/author/wandaRobinson-author

BOOKS BY THIS AUTHOR

Mourning into Dancing: My Journey Through Separation and Divorce.

(2017, 2nd edition 2018, 3rd edition 2021)

Hidden Treasures: A Collection of Godly Inspirations to Bless Your Soul.
Volume I and Volume II

(1st edition 2018 and 2019) (2nd edition--2021)

Treasure Chest of God's Promises: Six Month Devotional—2020

God is in Control: A Devotional—2021

The PAPA TOM Series (A children's series for ages 1-55+)

Papa Tom and Muffler the Barn Kitten—2019

Papa Tom and the Knit Blankets—2021

Papa Tom and His Garden—2021

THOTZ N' DOODLZ: Coloring Pages for MOMS--2021

THOTZ N' DOODLZ: Activity Pages for TEENS--2021

Made in the USA
Columbia, SC
21 September 2023

23178040R00105